# STOP OVERTHINKING

## WORKBOOK TO LEARN HOW TO CONTROL YOUR THOUGHTS

### Chris Zen

**Copyright 2023 All rights reserved©.**

The contents of this book may not be reproduced, duplicated or transmitted without the direct written permission of the author. Under no circumstances shall the publisher be held liable for any legal responsibility or liability for any repair, damage or monetary loss due to the information contained herein, either directly or indirectly.

**Legal Notice:**

No part of the contents of this book may be amended, distributed, sold, used, quoted or paraphrased without the author's consent.

**Disclaimer Notice:**

The information contained herein is for educational and entertainment purposes only. No warranties of any kind are expressed or implied. Readers acknowledge that the author does not render legal, financial, medical or professional advice.

# INDEX

| | |
|---|---|
| Foreword | 7 |
| Gratitude is the engine of happiness | 13 |
| Contact now | 17 |
| Positivity | 21 |
| Meditation | 25 |
| No comparison | 31 |
| Criticism and complaint | 37 |
| Awareness of the unconscious | 41 |
| Pleasure for pleasure's sake | 47 |
| Choose your battles | 53 |
| High vibration | 61 |
| Order | 65 |
| Positive discomfort | 69 |
| Help someone today | 73 |
| Less is more | 77 |
| Abundance | 83 |
| Neutral interpretation | 87 |
| Law of attraction | 91 |

Think less, feel more                    95

Final reflection                          99

# FOREWORD

First of all, I would like to welcome you to this book which, from now on, is yours. My deepest congratulations for having the courage and willingness to invest time in your personal development and inner peace. Few are those who dare to break out of their comfort zone and want to go further, so bravo to you. You are a great warrior with much to contribute to yourself and to all those around you.

**Overthinking is something that happens when we are distracted.** That is when we are not in the present moment. But what does that mean? If we think more than we feel, we are absent from the now; if we live anxious about the past or worried about the future, we are filled with anxiety, sadness, guilt, anger, resentment and we think too much.

The point is that our brain does not differentiate between imagination and reality. It feels exactly the same when something happens in your real life as it does when you imagine it. So start taking that power into account to use it to your advantage. Most of the things we worry about don't happen or don't become as bad as we had imagined. So, instead of worrying, get busy. Instead of reacting, we must act. Of course, I am referring to a negative reaction of course.

You may think that some of this book's chapters or concepts are unrelated to the main objective of stopping overthinking. But they all contribute directly in some way to your well-being and peace of mind and will help you to focus your attention on the here and now, to gradually reduce the noise of mental interference and give you the calm and balance we all need.

I want to tell you that none of the keys that I share with you in this book are unknown to me. Each and every one of them I have known, assimilated, tested and incorporated into my life over the years, because of their great effectiveness and positive effect, through my own experience, out of necessity, curiosity and will. In fact, many of these techniques and concepts, I still practice them often or from time to time in my day to day life, since there is always something we can improve or learn to be happier, healthier, creative and grateful.

I would not have the little courage, nor the little coherence to offer you something without knowing if it works because what good would that do you? And what good would it do me? What do I get out of showing the world something that I do not know if it is real, or if it is useful?

If someone taught me something, I tried it, it worked for me and I found it useful, it is my moral duty to pass that knowledge on to the next person, so that it is never lost. Likewise, there will be other knowledge that I discovered myself, or methods already learned from other people that I versioned to adapt to me, so that I can adapt myself to them.

There are many of these techniques or experiences that are related to each other, and that complement or influence each other, at least in a certain way. Having internalized and practiced some of these insights, you will find that your perspective has changed, that you can observe previously overlooked details, and how that which was previously unknown or incomprehensible about the world or yourself, now feels clear, crystalline and easy to understand or practice.

---

*"The mind that opens to a new idea never returns to its original size."*

## Albert Einstein

I myself, some time ago, could not understand certain concepts that I am now showing. I was just beginning my path of personal and spiritual development and there was a lot of new information to absorb. And I still have a lot to learn, fortunately. But that's what life is all about, and it's such a good teacher that if you don't learn a lesson, it repeats it again, and again and again, until you learn it.

The good thing about incorporating any of these techniques or concepts to our daily routine is that from the moment we assimilate them and start practicing them, we will see changes in us at different levels. For example: exercising improves health, but also calms your mind and positives your soul. Meditating calms your mind and reduces blood pressure, improving your circulation, concentration, positivity, etc. And so it is with each chapter of this book, we can cause a very powerful and positive ripple effect that will help us improve on all levels.

Sincerity is the real connection between hearts. This book is the bridge between my life and yours. One of the best and most beautiful forms of communication between people and cultures. I will not be the one to challenge the future of that bridge or compromise its endurance.

That is why I owe it to my word, values and consistency to offer you information worth sharing and using for your benefit.

When I realized that this information was valid for me, that it worked and helped me when I needed it most, I thought I should share it with more people. But, as we all know, very few people allow themselves to be helped unless they explicitly ask for it. It seems as if it would be an offense to accept someone's help. It would almost be like acknowledging that you couldn't solve it yourself, like publicly confirming that you didn't have the knowledge they wanted to give you, or like stating that you needed help and, of course, that could be considered as "weakness" in this world we live in.

But my friends, we are all more or less knowledgeable of a minimum of information in life and completely ignorant of almost everything else. In other words, masters of almost nothing, learners of everything. And why is it so hard for us to recognize that? Because of pride, dignity, appearances? I don't know what the most common reason is, but it seems absurd to me. We all, and I repeat, we all, need or could use the right help at the right time, or do we think that the biggest millionaires in the world, supposedly the most "successful" men on the planet, managed to get where they are completely alone and without anyone's help? No sir, I don't believe it.

*"If you walk alone, you will go faster; if you walk together, you will go farther".*

### Chinese proverb

Therefore, I believe that we must lower our guard from time to time, at least when it comes to learning, letting ourselves be influenced, silencing the ego and letting others speak. We have to learn to listen without wanting to respond. We must learn to listen in order to understand. To put ourselves in the shoes of the speaker and assimilate his or her experience.

And we have to doubt, to doubt everything we have learned and even ourselves, in order to be able to evolve and acquire new knowledge. This is the only way to achieve evolution and advancement of almost any kind. Thanks to the assimilation of new information that, together with the combination of your DNA and your other experiences and data, will give rise to new techniques and a fruitful development of your being and your environment.

Dare to know your maximum state of well-being. An optimal, maximum state, where your body will be light and resistant, your energy will be fluid and overflowing, your mood will be positive and joyful and your life will feel different, full of happiness and abundance.

Let us let ourselves go. Let us stop wanting to be and let us be. Let us stop thinking so much and let us feel. Here and now, all is well. At this moment, in silence, there is nothing wrong. If we already let the mind participate, it clutters the room. And then it is difficult to find what is no longer in its place.

*"The mind is like a parachute, it only works if it opens."*

**Albert Einstein**

# GRATITUDE IS THE ENGINE OF HAPPINESS

Gratitude is something that is within everyone's reach. It does not require great effort or much investment of time, but it can change our life and our perception of it absolutely radically.

By being grateful, we educate the mind to be aware of all the good surrounding us. We are focusing on the good. We are being able to highlight the many positive things in our life.

Surely many of us have heard that *"what you focus your attention on is what you attract or expand in your life"*. But surely we have all, all of us, heard the saying *"misfortunes never come alone"*. Isn't it funny? They are like two sides of the same coin. If I focus on the bad, more bad things will come. If, on the other hand, I focus on the good, good things will happen. And if you or someone around you really can't see the good things around you, you should look more closely. Or change the eyes with which you look.

We may think that there are no good things happening, or that there is nothing positive right now that we can notice. But that's not the case. You are here. You are alive, and that's already an amazing thing. You can breathe on your own, and that's a fascinating fact. You can read these lines; you had breakfast this morning, you slept warm, someone wished you good morning, you could take a shower with soap and water, you came back from work, you have money to cover your needs, you had a delicious dinner last night, you can walk using your two feet, etc. Do you still think there is nothing positive in your life?

We don't need to compare ourselves with other people's lives. In fact, it is unpleasant as the saying goes, but let's do it for a simple moment. How many people in the world are poor? How many are starving, cold, and suffering in the middle of a war? And, in spite of all this, they have on their beautiful faces the biggest and brightest smile possible? Wow... it is something to meditate on calmly. They, who have "so little" and we who have "so much"... They smile and go barefoot in the mud, we cry from our "palace". Depression, boredom and laziness are problems of the West, of the first world. They are problems caused by excesses. By the excess of superficial and fleeting pleasures, by the excess of empty and perishable stimuli, and by the excess of comfort. Yes, comfort. Routine and comfort, enemies of creativity and human evolution. Creators of the lack of values and appreciation of our lives and our environment.

The more we have, the more we want. And, the more we want, the less we value.

---

*"It is not he who has the most who is richest, but he who needs the least."*

## St. Augustine

---

It's not a matter of having too little. Or maybe it is. It is more a matter of valuing what you have or what you are. It is not having what you want, it is wanting what you have.

When you are able to see the infinite abundance that surrounds you, all is well. Everything is enough. Everything is a blessing, a fortune, a luck, a gift, a treasure. And you are the lucky one who can enjoy it. You just need to remove the blindfold from your mind, and stop comparing yourself to those who you think have "more" than you. Take a look at the chapter *"Pleasure for the sake of pleasure"* to understand that all that glitters is not gold. Not all "rich" people are happy. But you can be happy by being grateful. You can be "rich" without being a millionaire. You can feel the fortune of immense abundance in your life, sitting in the park feeling the sun on your face. Or walking in the rain with your pet on a Sunday. Or swimming in the sea or the pool feeling your body float lightly disobeying gravity.

Brother, you are alive! We are here and that's already a wonderful feeling, isn't it? Tell your mind to take a vacation and focus your attention on the here and now, aren't there countless reasons to give thanks today? Give thanks then. To the universe, to God, to Buddha, to Allah. To your mother, your father, your daughter or son, your brothers or sisters. To your neighbor, to the baker, to your co-worker. In solitude or in company. Say it, feel the power of gratitude. Notice how, when you feel, when you express gratitude and externalize it, the universe returns its energy immediately and the hairs on your body stand on end. And all this is not only because you want to attract good things, but also so that you can see all the good things that are already in your life without waiting for them.

Exercise:

*When we get out of bed, let's do a simple exercise. After going to the bathroom or brushing our teeth and drinking water, let's sit down in a place where we are comfortable. Close your eyes and place your right hand on your heart. Take a couple of slow, deep breaths and feel your body. Now, give thanks for everything you wish for. For what you feel you are blessed or fortunate to have or to be. Give thanks for your life, for food, for your home or your job, for your family and friends, for your health, for having improved as a person or for wanting to improve, for being generous or determined, for being sincere or sensitive, or simply give thanks for wanting to give thanks.*

*The instant feeling should be very positive. We are giving our whole organism, body, mind and soul, the powerful message that we are grateful for everything around us. Every cell in our body receives the information that we are happy and surrounded by abundance. That is a wonderful thing. And it is a cycle that feeds positively on itself.*

*Repeat this exercise for a month and observe the changes in your behavior, attitude towards others, or problems or situations that usually affect you negatively. I know it will help you see everything with different eyes and reinforce your attitude of positivity and strength.*

This exercise will change the perspective with which we see life and will positively program your subconscious so that, little by little, the unconscious and automatic thoughts of our mind are more and more positive, and do nothing but reaffirm our happiness.

# CONTACT NOW

"Live in the now." "Carpe diem." "Seize the moment." "Enjoy life." We have all heard these advertising sayings, but can we carry them out?

We live in an age where we are bombarded by stimuli and information, where there are hundreds, if not thousands of ways to access new "knowledge" instantly and from almost anywhere in the world.

But is that a good thing or a bad thing? They say that everything is bad in excess and in most cases, this is usually the case. Personally, I think that too much information is a bad thing, because two things happen:

**First:** the information received is not valued at all, since there is so much and it is so quickly consumed that it comes and goes in the blink of an eye. While we are trying to process it, we are already receiving the next one.

**Second:** they totally abstract us from the present moment. They are a continuous distraction and although sometimes this technology or information brings us closer to those loved ones who are far away, it also distances us from those who are close to us. In this way, we become absent from the now, which is the only thing that really "belongs" to us.

*Let's imagine for a moment a little girl born into a wealthy family. Every year, on her birthday, at Christmas, she receives an immense amount of gifts, of all shapes and colors, with no expense spared. Her parents want their daughter to have the best and to lack nothing, or perhaps they believe that this is a good way to raise their daughter, surrounded by a supposed abundance, even if it is only material.*

*In most cases, the child will grow up spoiled and without the ability to appreciate anything. She has had so many stimuli and gifts that she soon tires of them all. She needs more and more sensations to keep feeling that pleasure she gets from opening a new gift or buying a new pair of shoes. It's all about hormones and the effect they have on the human brain. That dopamine rush goes away as fast as it came and after a while, you feel the emptiness and need more and more, so you don't have to stop and analyze what is happening to you. It is certainly an addiction and a very common problem these days. We will talk more about this subject later in the chapter "Pleasure for pleasure's sake".*

*Now let's imagine the opposite case: a little girl born into a humble family bordering on poverty, where everyone helps out with the housework, where they are extremely lucky if they manage to put food on the plate once or twice a day for the whole month. The little girl loves to help her parents. They don't have a TV, so she spends her time talking to her mother, reading and playing with her only doll, which is now several years old and broken and unstitched. If, luckily, her mom and dad save a little money on her birthday and give their little girl a new doll, imagine her surprise! She will jump for joy, run around the living room and hug her parents, crying with joy and thanking them. Because this child is not used to this kind of stimuli, she does not live unconsciously, consuming without control, but her mind is in the now and she lives in the present without distractions or empty pleasures. Therefore, she values what she is given, what happens to her, and what she lives with her parents. This child will possibly be a great person and will be happy with little or even less.*

That is what happens to us with our present. We are exposed to so many stimuli and so much information that comes to us through our cell phone, social networks, email, calls, movies, series, work, news and press... that, for example, having dinner with our partner no longer seems important or worthwhile. That is because we live distracted, absent, overloaded with empty stimuli, with unbalanced dopamine, living on autopilot. And, in fact, what we overlook may be what really matters most.

The big advertising companies do not earn anything if you are happy. They win if you consume, if you feel fleeting and ephemeral "happiness" or, better said, pleasure, when buying and consuming their products. But, if you are happy, brother, no broken pants or old cell phone can take that away from you.

If you establish a solid foundation for your happiness, your life will be stable and purposeful, without needing external stimuli to motivate it temporarily or falsely.

And you won't need the latest cell phone, or the fashionable T-shirt, or the famous actor's cologne or the car they advertise on TV. You will already be happy and complete. And, if you ever decide to buy any of those things, you will enjoy and value them for what they are, something fleeting and material that does not define your identity, nor does it have anything to do with your happiness.

Exercise:

*When you feel distracted, angry or above all when negative thoughts assail you, touch the nearest wall. Breathe deeply and slowly as you do so. Now focus your attention on what you feel: is the wall cold or hot, smooth or rough, what do you feel when you touch it, firmness, control, support?*

*And now, tell me where is that negative thought or anger that consumed you?*

This is a good way to educate our mind so that it does not miseducate us. It is a way of showing her that there are certain things she thinks we don't like and that we don't plan to pay attention to her when she reminds us of them.

How else do you think the great men and women of success have become so by listening to their fears, insecurities and negative thoughts? I don't think so.

*"While no one can go back and make a new beginning, anyone can start now and make a new ending."*

## Carl Bard

Let us reflect for a few moments: now is when everything happens, when we can do something for our future, when we must do things that make us proud today and tomorrow, even more so. Don't wait for them to tell you the movie of your life, be the director, the actor and the scriptwriter.

*"There are only two days in the year when you can't do anything. One is called yesterday and the other tomorrow. Therefore, today is the ideal day to love, to do, to grow and, above all, to live."*

## Dalai Lama

# POSITIVITY

*"You have to be positive,"* they say. But sometimes it can be quite difficult. Especially in the days, we are living lately. That is why it is more important than ever that we learn to create, to feel and spread positivity, and to have it as our main attitude towards life, because it can help us in more than one and in more than ten moments a day.

Not everything goes as planned, or rather not often. There are different outcomes than expected, and the consequences are often not pleasant if they are beyond our control. At least, that's how we are used to seeing it. But how many times have we heard the saying *"every cloud has a silver lining"*, haven't we? And, from my point of view, there is a lot of truth in that saying, because many good things happen after events that we interpret as "bad".

*"My car broke down."* Of course, that's a bummer: the mechanic has to be paid and we'll have to get another method of transportation while it's being fixed, or we'll have to get out of bed a little earlier to use public transportation to get to work on time. But, if we keep our positivity and try to keep our vibe high, maybe after dropping the car off at the garage, instead of rushing into the subway and forgetting about it, you decide to enjoy the moment and relax, and treat yourself to breakfast at a coffee shop you've never seen before, and suddenly you run into an old classmate you haven't talked to in ages! You reminisce about old times, catch up and, magically, an opportunity arises to participate in a joint business project. Wow! Incredible, isn't it? Good thing my car broke down!

Or let's take another example: *You're at work serving customers, you've been there for five years and today looks like just another day on the calendar. Doing the same old operations, saying almost the same phrases, bored or* unmotivated... But, if you suddenly get out of the loop you're in, pay a little attention to the present and try to be more pleasant than usual, or ask the customer about his life or his day, magically everything is transformed! Instantly, everything becomes much more interesting and enjoyable; you talk about everything and anything, find things in common, crack a few jokes and laugh and you barely know each other! Maybe it will also give you some new contacts with whom you could expand your business. And it's all thanks to trying to be positive and paying attention to the present moment.

It is true that there are many thoughts that arise spontaneously from our mind and over which we cannot have any control, at least for the moment, but what we can choose to do is to pay attention to them or not.

*"If you don't like something, take away the only power it has: your attention."*

## Carolina Herrera

Exercise:

Whenever something bad crosses the thin curtain between your subconscious and your conscious, when you have noticed it arising, ignore it. Get on to something else. Sweep, sing, exercise, play loud music and dance. Humming works for me. My mind whispers something bad or negative, and I start humming whatever it is. A made-up tune, a familiar tune, anything. "Nana nananaaa nana nana naaa..." and suddenly, it's gone. The bad thought is gone. It got tired of you not paying attention to it and left. You've won this battle, but the war goes on. The difference is that you now have the right defensive strategy to come out unscathed. Non-resistance, acceptance, feeling more and thinking less.

I listen to what the mind says and if it doesn't bring me anything good, I'm not interested, so I divert my attention to something else. I smile, make today's to-do list or start warming up for exercise. We will talk more about this knowledge in the chapter "Present Contact".

Another technique to re-educate our mind is the following: every time you feel, or rather, think, something negative or that does not bring anything positive to you or to others, observe it. Analyze it. Ask yourself the following questions and answer right here in your book if you feel this way:

Exercise:

Why do I think that?

Do I really think so or is it just a meaningless outburst and not what I think or what I would like to do?

Is such thinking constructive or destructive?

Does or will it do any good, to me or to others, for me to say that thought out loud or to turn it into an action?

And, for me, the most important of all:

If I am watching that thought appear, then who is thinking it?

We confuse our mind with our identity and, from my point of view, this is a big mistake. Our subconscious governs our mind, and our subconscious is governed by the accumulation of experiences and knowledge acquired throughout our lives. There are images, concepts, rules or facts that are engraved in our subconscious and of which, for the most part, we are unaware of their existence. But they greatly influence the way we act, react, judge and live our lives. I think that is more than enough reason to want to continue researching more on the subject. Especially if we know that there is some unconscious impulsive behavior or attitude that does us or those around us no good, it is the ideal time to learn. To observe, analyze, accept, practice and improve.

---

*"The wound is the place where the light enters."*

## Rumi

---

Or in other words, every experience we have the potential to give us the learning we need. But only if we are alert. Humble and attentive, the world opens wide and shows us its infinite possibilities. And, remember, if there is any language in common with the rest of the people on this planet, it is the smile.

Don't you think it's worth the effort and focus on being positive?

# MEDITATION

What would you think if I told you that you have the possibility, the power and the strength to increase your well-being and health by changing your mind? Sounds great, doesn't it?

We can reduce the stress and burden of everyday life thanks to meditation. We forget the worries that accompany us and when we face them again, we do it with different eyes. We are giving ourselves the opportunity to reconnect with our inner nature, where calm and well-being reign.

*"The Buddha was asked: what have you gained from meditation? He replied: nothing. However, I tell you that I have lost anger, anxiety, depression, insecurity, and fear of old age and death."*

**Buddhist wisdom**

## Changes in our organism through meditation

Reduces blood pressure, inducing a state of calm.

Activation of certain parts of the brain related to love, empathy and compassion.

It improves our coordination and concentration, our memory and emotional stability.

Decrease symptoms of anxiety and depression.

There are already numerous scientific studies that support this type of practice. Thanks to brain scan tests, scientists can clearly observe the areas of the brain that are affected during meditation. And the results are fantastic and absolutely positive. So there is now scientific evidence and irrefutable proof that practicing meditation gives us the power to change our minds. And for the better.

## Other positive changes caused by meditation

Improves our ability to sleep easily.

Relieves muscle tension.

Decreases the production of cortisol, the fear and stress hormone.

It reduces the chances of getting cancer by oxygenating the body.

It helps us to disconnect and relax the mind.

Improves our overall health.

I really believe that we should practice meditation often, from an early age. Because the changes in our quality of life and in the way we relate to others would be spectacular, not only at the individual level. Surely, society would evolve positively in its interaction with nature and would devote more care to the impact it leaves on the environment. We would possibly take better care of ourselves; we would also feed ourselves in a more conscious way, we would follow an alkaline diet without causing so much pain to billions of animals in farms and industrialized processes.

And only thanks to a few minutes a day dedicated to you, to be in silence, to cultivate calm and forget the stress. Doesn't sound so complicated, does it?

## First step to meditate

Nobody is born knowing. At some point, we will have to start and learn, as everybody did. The learning process is a precious thing; it helps us in our evolution and prepares us better for the events to come.

Enjoy this novel experience that can give you many benefits to improve your health and well-being in a natural way.

It is as simple as sitting with your back straight while listening to relaxing music, best without lyrics. Breathe slowly and deeply and enjoy your moment of peace while trying to feel more and think less. It is not a matter of not thinking and feeling bad for doing so since that is automatic. It is a matter of, once a thought arises, not paying attention to it and being able to focus our attention on the music, on our body, on our breath. You can also help yourself at the beginning with aromatherapy or essential oils.

Below, I show you different variations of meditation for you to start practicing:

Ways to practice meditation:

**Looking at an image:** simply observing a photo, a drawing or the wall itself. Breathing slowly and deeply, we will achieve a state of relaxation and calm.

**Listening to or reciting a mantra:** energy is vibration, and music is vibration. One of the objectives of meditation is to raise our vibration, so listen to relaxing music or recite mantras, and you will get that positive and peaceful energy you are looking for.

**Concentration on the breath:** this is the most common of all, or the best known, but each person usually feels better in one type of meditation. Just feel the air coming into you when you inhale and the air going out when you exhale. Concentrate on its trajectory, on the sensation you receive, on the whole feeling.

Again I remind you: the important thing to see results, as in everything, is perseverance. Little by little, we will see incredible changes in our way of being and acting, and very good changes, you have my word.

These are some of the basic types of meditation. But there are other different ones and also combinations between them; the point is that all of them require deep breathing and a quiet environment without distractions where you can practice.

Start practicing meditation:

**Practice by yourself:** just do some research, feel, try the different modalities, you will see that it is very interesting.

**Read a book or watch a video tutorial:** we live in the information age, you have hundreds of possibilities to access the knowledge you are looking for, and you just have to start.

**Consult a friend who knows how to meditate:** surely, you know someone who knows someone who meditates. If you want to achieve something, there are no excuses.

**Participate in a course:** there are hundreds, if not thousands, of different courses of meditation and consciousness that are given in different parts of your country. Find out more and give it a try. You have very little to lose and much to gain.

## Pranayama Meditation

I want to show you one of the meditations that I have liked and worked the most since I started practicing. It is a type of Pranayama meditation, and it is very simple.

Exercise:

*Simply sit cross-legged, back straight but shoulders relaxed. Cover one of your nostrils as you slowly inhale through the other nostril. Now uncover that side and cover the side you took a breath in through. Exhale slowly through the free side and, without rushing, breathe back in through the side you breathed in through. Change sides. And so on.*

*Slow and deep breaths, enjoying the calm and silence that surrounds us.*

This breathing method balances our two brain hemispheres, just like pronouncing the famous OM in a mantra. In that way, we will balance our energy more easily and achieve a great state of relaxation without problems.

## Meditation in action

Little by little, you will notice that you are calmer, sleep better and don't get stressed as easily. Or maybe you're no longer in such a hurry to get to work, and instead, you're enjoying the road or the music on the radio more.

Exercise:
*You can put this technique into practice at any time of the day; it will help you relax your mind, calm anxiety and stress, and also improve your concentration and your ability to make decisions.*

*When negative thoughts come automatically or unconsciously, simply feel your body, be aware of it, breathe deeply and feel the air entering you. Pay attention to the sensation of your arms, your feet, and your body in general.*

And suddenly, the negative thinking is gone. It's gone. You've won this battle, but now you're ready for war. That is if you seek peace. Or so they say, right? Have a great day and enjoy the precious adventure of meditation, brother or sister. Peace.

# NO COMPARISON

From an early age, we get used to compare ourselves with others. It is something almost unconscious and automatic, an impulse of our behavior that really does not contribute anything positive to our life or to our happiness.

Many classmates had a toy and you didn't, so you would go crying to mom or dad to buy it for you. You had to be like them; you had to have what they had because you would feel different if you didn't. Wow... different! What a terrible thing to be different, isn't it? That's what we've thought all our lives, or what we were made to think.

If you were good in literature and languages, but bad in mathematics, they put you in a math reinforcement class, so that you would have the same level as the others, so that you would not be different from others. But, from my point of view, that is nonsense. No one is the same as anyone else, no matter how hard they try to be. There are different types of intelligence and the vast majority of us only have some intelligence in one thing or another, not in all, so we are different. So what's the point of trying so hard to be the same? It is the most effective way to lose your identity and to stifle creativity, to make you forget the talent and skill that life gave you in one field or another.

If someone is bad at math and good at literature, don't put them in a remedial class in math, but in literature! This is the only way to develop their potential in that which differentiates them from others. If we pretend to resemble others, we run the risk of achieving it, and then, when we achieve what that person had, if we do it at all, do you think it will fulfill you, is that what you wanted to achieve or what the person you wanted to resemble wanted?

If you behave as someone you are not, you will attract what does not suit you. You will attract what suits your character, your disguise, not your true essence.

From the time we are young we seek to integrate, be part of something, feel supported and socialize. None of this is bad except that we lose our identity. Almost all of us unconsciously forge an armor that protects us from the "attacks" of the outside world. We pretend to be tough and insensitive so as not to show any weakness and not to be an easy prey. It is sad but true, depending on the area, country and conditions in which you grew up, this is true to a greater or lesser extent. It is a form of self-protection, of emotional survival, it is something that is not said, but practically we all do it, at least in the first world.

If you show what you feel, they can use it against you, if you tell too much about yourself, they will envy and judge you, etc. Even people, when they cry in some event, program or similar, ask for forgiveness! Even people, when they cry in some event, program or similar, they ask for forgiveness! Forgiveness for what? For being alive, for feeling? I find it sad that a person should be ashamed for feeling, for showing their "vulnerable" side. The way I see it, crying or acknowledging your sensitivities doesn't make you weak, it makes you strong and real, mature and aware, and I see nothing wrong with that. If I watch a movie or documentary with a hard or tender scene that makes me feel, I cry and I don't care who is in front of me, if it's my partner or a theater full of people.

Feeling is good, it is beautiful, it is human, and it allows you to value life from other points of view and to observe those small details that make the present great, but, above all, feeling differentiates you from a world that, at times, can be hostile and cold.

Recognizing yourself with your quirks and flaws, with your virtues and talents, is one of the most rewarding processes there is. After throwing away your armor, you will be able to see the world with your true eyes; you will be able to attract what suits your true self, not your shell.

We are equally different, similar but different and all of us, believe me, all of us, are weird. What is this world's mania for us to be normal? Nobody is! If you spend your time and efforts trying to be like others, you will forget to be yourself; if you waste your life comparing yourself with others, you will not be able to appreciate how much you evolved and how much you learned during the whole process.

---

*"Facing panic is powerless, there is no competition, only against your version of yesterday."*

## Indian Wolf

---

What's more, comparing yourself to others is one of the most effective ways to prevent happiness from taking root in your life. Because you will be thinking about what you don't have and that person does have, but she went through another process to get it, and it will probably mean something very different to her than it does to you. We can't compare ourselves to anyone simply because we are not like anyone else. We weren't born or raised on their terms; we didn't get the same upbringing or have the same parents, the same DNA, the same mentality or way of seeing or doing things. So why would I want what that person has out of greed or envy?

**If I want to be someone else, so be it! But then be a better version of yourself, not the same version someone else is.**

If you don't like something about yourself, change it; if you can't, accept it. And what you like about yourself, work on it, improve it, expand it, make it your signature and your seal. If you compare yourself with someone, do it to learn something good, not to envy them or feel bad about your current situation.

*"Be yourself. The rest of the roles are already chosen."*

## Oscar Wilde

I know from my own experience that, by being oneself, relationships will become more sincere, friends more loyal and affectionate and life more happy and abundant.

Woe to him who confuses his disguise with his identity, his mind with his true self, and his ego with his essence. We are; we do not think we are. Of course, if I want to be one way or another and do what is necessary, I will eventually end up being that way, but that is not what I mean now. I mean that we are more feeling than thinking, more being and giving than having, more now than before or after, more present and aware than distracted and absent.

Exercise:

*This exercise is very similar to the one proposed in "Criticism and Complaint" chapter. It is simple, when you perceive that you are mentally or verbally comparing yourself with someone, stop. Observe yourself. Ask yourself the reason for this attitude. Maybe it's envy, jealousy, frustration. None of that is positive. Stop and breathe. Look at your life and everything you've accomplished to get here. You have a home, food, friends, health, and surely much more... and it's already more than most of our human brothers and sisters on the planet have.*

*And are we going to be the ones who don't value what we have? No. Absolutely refuse to let yourself be carried away by those thoughts that bring nothing good. Just by the fact that you were born, you are already a winner. You were chosen among hundreds of millions and you managed to reach the egg, enter, create life and be born.*

*You are great. However you are, you are great. Repeat it with me "I AM GREAT". Again, I want to hear it right "I AM GREAT".*

*Now with passion, one more time, "I AM GREAT". Now go out there and succeed. The world is yours.*

# CRITICISM AND COMPLAINT

*"What a day!", "stupid, look where you're going!", "that guy is a...", "I don't want to go to work", "I have to do that and I can't stand it", "I hate my job, but that's what it is",* etc.

These and hundreds, or rather, thousands of other criticisms and complaints, much louder and with worse words, are what we are used to hearing or saying, day, after day, after day. In fact, there are even popular phrases and sayings that contain more than one negative word or phrase and, inexplicably, are part of our culture.

They really are a waste of energy. Literally.

If I spend even a small part of my time remembering how much I don't like my job, I will feel bad just for saying it, and I will feel that way from the moment I say it until I leave the office or my job and stop working. And during the whole process, we will have created a mental reminder that is telling us: *"I don't like this", "what a piece of crap", "why am I not able to look for something else?"* and other condescending, self-pitying and emotionally devastating phrases.

While it is true that it is normal to be annoyed by something or many things in our daily lives, there are ways and means to deal with it, or rather, there are two ways to act: either accept it or change it.

If it is something that I cannot change, and I already know that I do not like it, why give it more time in my life? Why affirm our dislike with words? That will only reaffirm our discomfort and will not solve anything, but rather make it worse. It will make the task much longer and more tiring, the hours will go on forever and the ticking of the clock will slow down even more than usual.

It may seem like we are letting off steam and releasing ballast, but, in my opinion, we are reaffirming and consolidating that bad feeling and giving it power over us, negatively altering our energy, vitality and positivity.

We must take into account the power of our words, since what we externalize with words, has the power to affect us positively or negatively. Let us not allow something that does not feel good to stay in our lives longer than necessary. We deserve better. You deserve better.

Even today, I still catch myself in the middle of a complaint and before saying an unpleasant qualifying adjective, I shut up in mid-sentence, or end it with *"I don't like it"*, instead of using a disqualifying or rude adjective, full of anger and in which we will invest part of our time and energy that we will never get back.

Little by little, we are training our subconscious to make it understand that we do not like complaints and criticisms, they are useless and we will not dedicate even a second more in our lives to them. In this way, we will be able to stop the constant flow of negativity that can come out of our mind unconsciously and automatically.

Exercise:

*Whenever you realize that a complaint or destructive criticism is about to come out of your mouth, stop. Analyze it. Observe yourself. Don't judge, don't express a negative word, don't give power over you to the "bad" that has already happened. Sing, hum, do push-ups, dance, or talk about what you have to do today. Change the chip. Radically change the subject of your mind. Don't let that negative feeling take root in your day.*

*And if you have already said that complaint, criticism or negative word, change the subject anyway, focus your mind on something else. Don't pay attention to it, don't develop it. Because even if the bad thing that has happened is not your* fault, you will end up paying the consequences. And even if you don't believe it or don't think so, it will have been your decision.

Yes, you can almost never decide what happens around you, but you can always choose how it "makes you feel" because you are the one who decides to feel that way. That's why I no longer say "that bothers me", "you make me nervous", etc. Because it is me who gets upset, it is me who gets nervous; it is me who, unconsciously, let myself be carried away by that impulse and decide, automatically or not, to surrender to that torrent of emotions and hormones that makes me feel strength after anger, security after criticism, power after the rejection of the unknown.

*"A disciple came very agitated to Socrates' house and said to him:*

*Master! I must tell you how a friend of yours was badmouthing you.*

*To which Socrates quickly replied: "Wait! Have you already passed through the three filters what you are going to tell me?*

*The three filters? -asked the student with surprise.*

*Yes," Socrates answered, "the first filter is the TRUTH. The first filter is the TRUTH. Do you know for sure if what you want to tell me is true from beginning to end?*

*No," replied the disciple, "I heard it from some neighbors.*

*Then at least you will have passed it through the second filter, KINDNESS. Tell me, is what you want to tell me good?*

*No, not really... it's the opposite.*

*Ah," exclaimed Socrates, "let's look at the last filter then. Do you NEED to tell me about it?*

*To be honest, it's not really necessary," the student replied.*

*Then," smiled the master, "if it is neither true, nor good, nor necessary, let's bury it in oblivion".*

## Text adapted from Socrates

This is how we should react when deciding whether to let a complaint or criticism about someone or something leave our lips and resonate in our being, modifying its vibration and affecting us negatively or positively.

When we are going to complain or criticize, let us ask ourselves the following questions: is it true, is it good, is it necessary?

Most of the time, if not all, destructive criticism, insults, complaints or victimhood are neither true, nor good, nor necessary.

Love yourself a little more and give yourself only good words that encourage and motivate you to be happier today, now. Use your words to your advantage, and don't allow negative emotions and feelings to transform the way you see things and reduce your chances of living a better life.

*"Don't let your wounds make you into someone you are not."*

## Paulo Coelho, Manuscript found in Accra, 2012.

# AWARENESS OF THE UNCONSCIOUS

Throughout the day, there are certain things we do automatically. They are unconscious reactions or impulses and don't need our permission to modify our behavior. They rest in a deep place in our mind waiting for the perfect moment to come out, creating a reaction that, at times, may not be the one we expected to have.

It takes time to change an unconscious reaction because it is part of the automatic programming we have received during our life. It is rooted in the deepest part of our mind and has conditioned us to react in a specific way, so much so that we already consider that reaction as an inseparable part of our being.

Humans are creatures of habit, and it is much more difficult to eliminate an already assimilated habit than to create a new one. That is why they say that, in the learning process, it is always more important to unlearn than to learn. But it is also more complicated at the same time.

Something that has been ingrained in us for years and years, forming part of our ideals and beliefs, is difficult to change because we must stand up to ourselves and tear down a whole structured system that forms our identity.

But today, we are not the same person who accepted those ideals yesterday. Nor will we be the same as we will be tomorrow, even if we are quite similar. Therefore, something that was useful or valid for us yesterday may not necessarily fit us at all today.

That can give us enough reasons to be able to question some of our behavior: do I want to be the same as yesterday's person who failed in certain situations, or do I want to continue as I am now in the present for the rest of my life? Or do I prefer to collect all that information gained through trial and error and be the best version of myself for tomorrow?

*"The best way to predict the future is to create it."*

## Abraham Lincoln

To build solid and stable happiness for tomorrow, we must work on it today, value our situation, feel gratitude. To improve our future physique, we must exercise today, eat healthy, not make our bad habits a habit. And so on.

If we don't like something on the outside, analyze within yourself why you don't like it. If it is something unfair or we witness an abuse, it is perfectly normal to be indignant, at least to some extent.

But if it is something more subjective, like the way your partner behaves, or the multiple messages from someone who needs your help, or how a car pulls into your lane without posing a great risk to your safety, and yet you still get angry or curse, yell or stay with discomfort inside, there is something inside you that you can improve today for your future well-being.

It is only when we become aware of the negative effects of certain unconscious behaviors in our lives and in the lives of those around us that we begin to ask ourselves certain questions. You can answer them right here as an exercise if you wish.

Exercise:

*If I make others or myself suffer with my reaction, shouldn't I try not to react that way?*

*Am I wrong to react this way? Why do I react this way?*

*Is it impatience, is it because I want everything done my way, maybe because I want to control everything?*

These types of questions can be very useful if what we really want is to eliminate an automatic negative behavior. That way, every time we lose our temper or get the blues, we can look inward to find the root of the problem.

Because in my opinion, when something "bothers you", it is not that something that is the reason for your anger; it is you that is bothered because of your perception of the situation. Then, to solve the problem, what must change is you, not the alleged problem.

You don't know how many unnecessary battles you can avoid like this, noticing that impulsive reaction is about to come out of you. Then you don't allow it; you analyze your feelings or thoughts and realize that the problem is not the problem but how you see the problem.

And believe me, we all have some internal detail that should be addressed; we are all weird in the eyes of others who are not familiar with that kind of weirdness.

There is no such thing as normality. At least, it sounds like a legend to me. I think the real problem is wanting to be normal or pretending to be normal, when in reality, you know that you are denying your true essence.

Be rare. Be authentic. Speak without filter. No harm, no foul, but no filter. Jump up and down. Shout for joy. Run. Give without expecting to receive. Eat something tasty. Laugh out loud. Call someone you haven't seen in a while and tell them you miss them. Say sorry, say thank you, and say I love you more often. And be thankful again and again for the wonderful fortune of being alive brother.

But let's get back to the matter at hand. We want to improve something about ourselves, something that doesn't do us or those around us any good. If you have already detected that behavior, reaction or unconscious impulse, you have already taken a big step. Only courageous beings are capable of confronting themselves and their defects in order to build a better version of themselves. Challenging your mental structure, which you have been functioning all your life, is challenging. But believe me, only good things can come out of it. Outside the comfort zone, in the positive discomfort zone, is where the real magic happens. It is where you will reach your greatest development, where you will flow free and light, where you will find yourself.

It's funny that you have to be uncomfortable to feel really comfortable, but I don't think we find the concept so strange or new. For example, after doing a hard workout, or finishing a months-long project, or managing to quit smoking after years of trying, we feel fulfilled. It is a moment of realization in which we are fully aware and in the present, living in the now with all our strength. We have achieved something great and after considerable effort and sacrifice. And how good it feels, doesn't it? What satisfaction, what happiness, how comfortable one feels after having achieved what took so much effort to achieve. After being "uncomfortable" for a long time, we achieved a great goal, but it was worth that temporary "discomfort" in exchange for a breakthrough in our life. And all thanks to being here, present, concentrated, focused on the now. Small step by small step, achieving great things. Let's value and understand the true power of being more conscious in our life and being positively "uncomfortable".

Exercise:

*Analyze what part of your behavior or reaction is impulsive or unconscious and negatively affects you or those around you.*

*Stop when you notice you've said something you didn't mean to say. Study yourself. Take two slow, deep breaths. Answer these questions right here on a piece of paper:*

*Why did I say or do that?*

*What did he intend to achieve by saying or doing that?*

*And did I succeed? So was it worth it to react like that?*

*If you have answered honestly, you will see what happened from another point of view. Look at the supposed reason why you decided to react this way. Is it real, or is it only your way of looking at it that makes you react this way? If we look inside ourselves when something feels wrong, we will be able to understand that, most of the time, the problem was not on the outside but in our way of seeing the outside.*

*Don't be angry with yourself. Accept yourself, take care of yourself, say out loud what you would like to hear to accelerate your healing and boost your motivation. You reacted according to the level of awareness you had at the time and that's it.*

Consciousness is the way to grab life head-on and make it yours. If you are conscious, you draw your life; if you live unconsciously, your life will draw you.

*"Until the unconscious becomes conscious, the subconscious will run your life, and you will call it destiny."*

### Carl Gustav Jung

First, we must be aware that there is something inside of us that can be improved. A defect, an attitude or something that does not contribute anything positive to our life. From that moment on, we isolate that behavior or reaction from ourselves and we are able to see what is happening. The process will not be finished yet, but we will certainly have made it start. In this way, we will make a kind of mental mark so that the next time that reaction appears, we will be able to notice it. Thanks to that, we will be able to prevent that attitude, behavior or sensation from developing more than necessary. Because, as it happens, we will be able to realize that this behavior does not belong to us and we will be able to return to a positive or neutral mental attitude.

And so, little by little, with the passage of time, this reaction will be limited until it reaches a point of not happening, since, consciously, we have been positively programming the unconscious, making it understand that we do not like this reaction because it does not take us anywhere and is of no use to us. The day will come when we will observe that our automatic reaction to certain events is not the same as it was months or years ago.

It is a process that takes perseverance, awareness and patience, but it is really worth the effort and will change our lives for the better.

# PLEASURE FOR PLEASURE'S SAKE

How delicious the food is, and how we love desserts! Or how good it feels to drink a beer on a terrace in the middle of summer, how we enjoy good sex, or smoking, shopping, earning and spending money.

Most of these things or activities are not negative at all, in fact, indulging in the "luxury" of having a few beers chatting with friends, or going shopping to feel pretty from time to time is recommended and even healthy.

No one is going to take care of you as well as you take care of yourself. Pampering yourself and giving yourself those moments for yourself is great; it's practically a necessity and a reward for our work or for simple enjoyment. Because we are not in this life just to work and pay bills and think about our worries and responsibilities. From time to time, we have to stop the train, get off and get some fresh air and feel the warmth of the sun on our faces. Think less and feel more. But that's not the point.

When I talk about pleasure for pleasure's sake, I am referring to basing your happiness exclusively on getting pleasure. That is, believing that you are happy for spending on unnecessary purchases or luxuries, or for earning more money, for having more sex, for feeling superior to someone... That is the real mistake, indeed, it is a real condemnation.

Because the moment will come when you have done everything or almost everything, and you will feel empty, unsatisfied, depressed, irascible, and you will pay for it with yourself or with your loved ones, and you will try to drown your sorrows in alcohol, overeating, drugs, sex, etc... And so it starts all over again.

*"The pursuit of pleasure leads to pain."*

## Herodotus

I have a friend who is a millionaire. And he, fortunately, is a positive, happy and grateful person. But he tells me that many of his friends, also millionaires, are either addicted to cocaine, sex, alcohol or prostitution or are lonely and depressed.

This is because they have confused pleasure with happiness. It is as simple as that but perhaps complex to understand. I will try to explain more clearly: pleasure comes from the outside; it is an external stimulus that gives us a pleasant feeling of well-being, a source of hormones that flood our organism and revolutionize it whether it is from unhealthy food, but with flavor enhancers, processed sugar and other artificial additives, or from money, drugs, power or sex. Pleasure is something that does not last. It comes, it stimulates us, and after a while, it is gone, just a faint memory of how good it was. And we will quickly need another dose to satisfy our thirst. It is a never-ending story.

*"Money is a number, and numbers never end. If you need money to be happy, your search for happiness will never end."*

## Bob Marley

However, happiness is something that comes from within. It is an attitude, a way of living. It is the journey, not the destination. It can be pouring rain outside; inside, we can feel a warm, sunny day. We don't need anything concrete to feel happiness; it's your way of seeing things that will make you feel happy. You don't have to wait for the storm to pass; you have to learn to dance in the rain.

They say that happy people are grateful, but I don't see it that way. I think it is grateful people who are happy. **Because if we value what we have, feel and are, everything around us will shine with a different color.** A rainy day will look nice because we will be at home warm or in good company; or when they change our work schedule, we will focus on what we can do by having a different shift, such as that pending task we wanted to accomplish; or if we have to work more, we can think that we will earn more money if we work more hours and what we can invest it in, etc.

*"Half of the beauty depends on the landscape; the other half, on the man who looks at it."*

## Lin Yutang

As we discussed in the chapter *"Gratitude is the engine of happiness"*, if we are aware of how privileged we are and how much abundance surrounds us, we will naturally feel immense joy.

This is precisely what I meant when I told you that pleasure is external and happiness is internal. When we keep in mind how fortunate we are, when we value our health, our life, our friendship or family relationships, when we appreciate the love of our partner or our pet, enjoy a sunny or rainy day, appreciate having a roof to shelter under, having a plate on the table, a job, good conversations or company and a long etc., then we will not need an external stimulus to feel happiness. The inner peace and gratitude that we will feel will be so intense that it will raise our energy to another level, and our perception of the world will change. We will look at the same sky with different eyes. We will walk the same path with different steps. The world will be the same, but we will have evolved. Suddenly, worries will be less worrisome, problems less serious, anger will be softened until it no longer exists, and smiles will be our new language.

*"If you don't change, everything repeats itself."*

## Anonymous

Happiness will be our natural and almost automatic state because we will have understood that the secret is not to have but to be. At the end of the day, it is about being happy and making those around us happy, and even in those moments when it seems that you are not doing well and you have a bad patch, when several problems or worries come together, even then, surely there is a lot to be grateful for.

Exercise:

*It is simple, I propose that we write on a piece of paper everything we know that does not do us any good, health-wise, emotionally or mentally, but nevertheless, we continue to give it a place in our lives. Take it out of you, externalize it and try to see it in an isolated or more objective way.*

*"If you know what you have to do and you don't do it, you're worse off than before."*

## Confucius

*Let's answer these questions honestly:*

*What does this bad habit or excess bring me?*

*Does that make me happier or a better person, or just pleasure me?*

*What would happen if I stopped doing it?*

*How else, in a less harmful and more natural way, can I get the same feeling you give me, or even a better, healthier, longer-lasting one?*

*Why don't I choose that option then?*

I am not here to judge you. I have been down this road, and it is my intention to show you the steps I followed that worked for me to stop being a slave to the mind, to bad impulses and to the unconsciousness that governs almost all of us to a great extent.

No one but you will read your answers, so try to be as honest as possible, so you can detect as soon as possible the root of the "problem" which is not such a thing but rather a life event produced by distraction or unconsciousness.

You can also share this information with your partner or loved ones, and they may help you look for concrete evidence to make the process easier and more enjoyable.

From time to time, it is very important to free ourselves from that burden that we assume we must carry alone and to express to our close people how we feel. In this way, we externalize the "problem" and everything is relativized and loses importance to some extent.

Let go of shame, pride or fear, and bring out that thing inside you that is blocking you.

Emptying your backpack of stones is a very healthy thing that can be good for all of us. Also, you will be aware that maybe you should not have accumulated so many and, later on, you may think twice before accumulating them again.

# CHOOSE YOUR BATTLES

There are many ways for there to be a misunderstanding; the possibilities are many: maybe I could not express myself as I wanted, I chose the wrong words or tone, or maybe the moment, the looks or the body expression also, if this message arrives by phone, email, cell phone message, etc. That is, if they read it, they only imagine how I said it and interpret it in their own way.

Maybe the other person had a bad day and was feeling bad and didn't have the patience at the time to stop and think about whether the words meant one thing or another. And because of the way your mind is structured and your learning as you grow up, it will also help you interpret it one way or the other.

So having a misunderstanding or argument over supposed differences is easier than it sounds, right? So why want to be right? Maybe both people are right or neither is! It's very relative and subjective, as everyone interpreted the words in their own way and perhaps, with no malicious intent on either side, a silly misunderstanding was reached.

There are several ways to know how to choose our "battles" or, better said, to avoid ego duels that lead nowhere and, in this case, as in many others, I base myself entirely on Buddhist wisdom:

- Don't be offended:

When some expression or attitude of someone bothers you or you feel offended, it is not their words that offend you; it is you who "decides" consciously or unconsciously to feel offended or get angry. Nothing offends you; you are offended. Because you don't agree, because it clashes with your ideals, because it's not how you would do it. However, you want to see it.

Don't resist or let the thought lead you to an unnecessary and possibly unjustified reaction. Accept it and ask yourself if it really is the way you see it or maybe, in a remote possibility, it could be otherwise and still be totally correct!

Obviously, you have to act whenever you can to avoid injustices and abuses but do not make it personal; take care and cultivate your inner peace.

Because if you take offense, you are consolidating and reinforcing that bad energy in you and ensuring that it lasts longer over time.

- Free yourself from the need to win:

*"Everybody talks about peace, but nobody educates for peace. People educate for competition, and competition is the beginning of any war."*

### Lipnisky

What for some is "losing", for others is learning. What for some is "winning", for others is enjoying. Wanting to win is a way for the ego to feel strong, and you must not let it affect or change you; otherwise, you will become someone cold and apathetic, who only seeks victories and titles to inflate his chest and boast of a beautifully adorned identity, but who is empty inside.

We have all won at one time or another, and we have all lost many more, and does that change you? In fact, maybe it is even more useful to lose than to win because at least losing leaves you with a beautiful learning from which you can nourish yourself, if you recognize that you can learn something, if you are willing and humble. But winning only feeds the ego; it only separates you from others. And the one who won today may lose tomorrow, so what? Will he be sad, frustrated and feel little? It doesn't make any sense! You are not what you have; you are what you do, what you feel and make you feel. Losing or winning doesn't define you, just try to observe without being a judge, enjoy without wanting to outdo anyone but your version of yesterday.

- Free yourself from the need to be right:

Most of the time, when we listen to someone, we prepare our response; we are loading ammunition to release our reasons or motives to prove that our argument is valid and adequate. It is our way of defending our presumed identity and wanting to differentiate ourselves from others. But we are already different. And also the same. We are equally different.

But we want to be right. We want to prove that we know more and better. But how absurd is this endless fight! Again I remember that we are all masters of almost nothing and learners of everything. We all know something about certain subjects and almost nothing about everyone else!

*"When you talk, you just repeat what you already know. But if you listen, you can learn new things."*

### Dalai Lama

By listening without thinking about responding, better said, by listening without thinking, just feeling the words the other person emits, their attitude and knowledge, we are allowing them to contribute to us, allowing part of the wisdom of their experiences to enter into us and enrich us. That is the beauty of life, diversity. And in the richness of difference is evolution.

Suddenly, by letting go of the ego's limiting beliefs, and by assuming that perhaps there are more truths besides my own, I am liberated. I grow. I allow a new stream of ideas to become part of my life, making it richer and more exuberant. Do not close yourself to the flow of knowledge that circulates the planet beyond your mind and allow yourself, from time to time, to doubt even yourself, to allow other realities to be and connect with you.

- Free yourself from the need to feel superior:

We have the habit of feeling above others, or rather the addiction. That may be the reason for so much useless criticism, so much envy or contempt for those who have more or who have less, who are different or who are similar to us. Whatever, the point is to feel powerful. By despising others, I don't have to face my fears, defects and insecurities that make me look for my strength in bad words and forms, in expensive cars and suits, in jewelry and other empty vices.

We are from the same place and we will see each other in the same place.

You just have to be better than what you were yesterday; you have to be a better version of you; that's the only person you have to compete against and want to surpass. Period.

- Free yourself from the need to have more:

To have, to have, to have. To satisfy our cravings, our ego to feel above others or part of the group. There are healthier ways to feel integrated than having the same as everyone else. If you want money, you'll always want more, if you're on a one-night stand, you'll never have enough, if you're obsessed with vices and pleasures, you'll eventually burn out and lose your meaning and reason for being along the way.

If you reach a goal, you will be thinking about the next one and waste your time of life, love and learning, thinking about the next title or trophy to put in your showcase.

Happiness is a journey, not a destination. It is to be, not to have.

There are more interesting Buddhist fundamentals, but these are the ones we will learn about today.

In short, if we learn not to feel offended, if we forget our false need to be right, to win or to feel superior, and if we accept that having more will not make us happy if we are incapable of valuing what we already have, then we will be FREE. Free from the influence of our ego, from the unconscious impulses that bring us nothing good, and free to know how to choose our battles correctly.

Enjoy and use these new superpowers wisely to create and maintain your inner peace.

*"Be the change you want to see in the world."*

**Mahatma Gandhi**

Write down here the concepts that have most caught your attention so far:

_____
_____
_____
_____
_____
_____

How do you plan to apply these concepts to your life?

_____
_____
_____
_____
_____
_____
_____

After writing these lines, read them aloud to begin to internalize

# HIGH VIBRATION

*"If you want to discover the secrets of the universe, think in terms of energy, frequency and vibration."*

## Nicola Tesla

According to the basic principles of quantum physics, we continuously exchange energy with our surroundings. Therefore, we had better make sure that what surrounds us is good and positive so that the energy that reaches us is enriching and useful, and also so that we do not run out of energy to use in our own development and evolution.

How many times have you just finished talking to a good friend and you feel great, bursting with positivity, gratitude and vitality! It's not happenstance. It's more like causality. Or remember those other times when you've just finished talking to someone negative, always criticizing others, envying, insulting and belittling every chance you get, and by the time you realize it, you're tired, low in spirits and don't feel like doing anything. I think we have all gone through that; the question is whether we realize what is happening.

There are people who give and there are people who take away; there are people with whom you share energy and leave you empty, dry, and withered. On the other hand, there are other people who renew you, strengthen you, and motivate you. We are energy and that is indisputable, but sometimes you have to observe these details to understand the concept, the power and influence that this can have in our lives.

If we are energy, and energy is vibration at a certain frequency, then we could say that we are energy in high or low vibration depending on the moment. Each feeling corresponds to a different vibration, the good ones are high frequencies and the bad ones are low.

There are many factors that can affect our vibration:

**Environment:** there may be more things around you that affect you than you could imagine. Having your home or workplace tidy and clean is not only to find things faster but to give calm and peace to your mind and soul, and not to receive chaotic energy from your environment.

**Music:** Music is vibration and energy just like us; when we listen to it, it can immediately raise or lower our frequency. Try to listen to positive, upbeat, or 432 Hz music when meditating or working to tune into the right frequency.

**Visual stimuli:** that information that enters through our retina through the ocular nerve to the brain is sedimented in our subconscious, sowing a seed that, sometimes, does not give the sweet fruits that we could expect. When we watch movies of violence, misfortune, or news that give us fear and mistrust, or advertising that motivates our consumerism and dissatisfaction with your partner, house, car or current physique, we are receiving signals that remain in the unconscious part of our mind and tell us that we could have more and better, that what we have and what surrounds us is not the latest, the most beautiful, the most expensive, the youngest. It seems innocent, but after years and years of receiving this contradictory information, the mind can play tricks on us and it may be difficult to detect what is the root of your dissatisfaction, especially if the cause has been catalogued as normal, since it is something we absorb daily.

**Company:** they say that we are the average result of the people around us. So let's surround ourselves with good people! We are of an age to choose our company, so let's select well. Positive, cheerful, grateful people will help us feel good and attract good things into our world. On the other hand, negative people, who live in constant complaint and criticism and constantly victimize each other, may not help us attract anything but bad things into our lives. Choose wisely.

Words: we should never underestimate the immense power of words. Our words can uplift or bring others down, just as we can be happy, saddened or angered by something said to us. Words carry a powerful charge of identity and intention that can move mountains, and it puts every cell in our body to work on that received energy. That is why we often feel bad just by imagining something that has not even happened because the word and the mind have an impressive and determining power in our lives. It is exactly for this reason that I repeatedly say that destructive criticism and complaints are useless because, even if that person or that fact deserves to be criticized, some of those bad words will splash us and contaminate our energy, thus reducing our vitality, positivity and effectiveness.

*"Modern science has not yet produced a soothing drug as effective as a few kind words are."*

## Sigmund Freud

Thoughts: last but not least, thoughts. The root of everything. The raw material to materialize our most pleasant dreams or our darkest nightmares.

In this book, we have different chapters that address the important task of "taking care" of our thoughts in different ways. *"Neutral interpretation", "Awareness of the unconscious", "Positivity", "Think less, feel more"*, are some of them.

Thoughts are electrical impulses that originate in our brain on a constant basis. And, if the whole universe is energy, imagine what happens to them. They are sent out as a vibration frequently into the universe and then come back to you in the form of facts or reasons for you to keep thinking that way. It is something like a mirror effect, or like throwing a stone into a lake. The ripples caused by the stone (thought) will expand omnidirectionally through its 360 degrees around it, being infinitesimally smaller and becoming imperceptible to us, but they run their course. And sooner or later, they will rebound and return to the source (our mind or life), materialized in the language (high or low vibration) that was emitted.

In short, if you think bad thoughts and pay too much attention to those negative thoughts frequently, you will receive more motives, facts and sensations that allow you to continue in that bad vibration. If, on the other hand, you decide to let those bad thoughts pass you by and only pay attention to the good ones, being aware and striving to live in the now with gratitude and love, good things will happen in your life to reinforce that thinking. It sounds a bit theoretical or crazy, but it really works, I can attest, and besides, what do you lose by trying it?

# ORDER

Over every form of existence on Earth, there is an order. Sometimes disorderly, sometimes senseless or chaotic, but there is an order, after all. Everything must follow a precise way of functioning and if sometimes this balance is broken, it causes a domino effect of negative consequences. But we humans believe that we live without being affected or dominated by that order. We feel we are masters of everything and above everything until everything passes over us. We are not safe from the rules that govern this universe. Let us remember; we are not in the universe, we ARE THE UNIVERSE. We are formed by the same matter and substances of the stars. If we manage to change our being, our dynamics, attitude and actions, we will inevitably change our environment.

But we forget our creative power. We live in a continuous madness of stimuli, distractions, emotions, and addictions that cloud our senses and take us away from our infinite potential. We are creators; we are creative, we are all or nothing. Of **course, we are absolutely linked to our environment by energy, and the energy to materialize our dreams in the real world is thought.** And it comes up most of the time spontaneously and we think we have a lot to do with what it says and sometimes we don't. We must find a way to affect our dreams in the real world positively. We must find a way to positively affect our subconscious so that those automatic, unconscious thoughts are more positive, calmer, logical, and productive. Otherwise, we will remain in a mere attempt to fully develop our potential and the mission or task we came here to fulfill.

Order is the way to make something work. It is the algorithm, the formula, the grandmother's cake recipe.

Find your order and you will find your balance and you will be able to show all your talent and skill on the game board.

I do not mean to have your room well placed when I talk about order, although it is also. If, according to quantum energy, energy flows from us and to us and surrounds us, if there are many elements out of place, they will impede the normal flow of energy and our renewal of vitality and creativity. In addition, seeing a tidy room relaxes the mind instantly, doesn't it? Although we have long been accustomed to seeing something messy, seeing it clean and tidy, the instant feeling is calm and restful, whether we want to see it or not. Again, I remind you that extremes are not good: it is not bad to have a messy room or kitchen from time to time, after a meal with friends or a day at work, nor is it healthy to be obsessed with cleanliness all day and suffer when you see a crumb of bread on the floor and lose your nerves, those of us who have pets know that. Simply and according to my point of view, having the habit of tidying up or not messing much is something very healthy and relaxing, as it gives us a nice space to rest and renew our energies and ideas.

Likewise, your life, your habits or tasks should be orderly, since it is the best way to achieve what you propose and to be at maximum productivity during the day, the week, the month...

### Issues to address to get your life in order

There are certain issues that block your true development that many of us have ingrained in us.

I would like to highlight the following:
**Fear of the new:** change can give a feeling of discomfort or rejection, perhaps because we are leaving our comfort zone and "moving away" from what we are used to, but leaving the comfort zone is, if not the only way, one of the most effective ways to achieve your goals and succeed.

**Overthinking:** this is something we talked about throughout this book and the previous episode of *"Guide to Better Living: Mind"*. Think less, feel more; that's one of the great secrets to unlocking your true hidden potential.

**Undervalue yourself:** don't think or say negative things about yourself because a part of you ends up believing them and reduces your energy, effectiveness, positivity and chances of success.

*"Speak not evil of yourself, for the warrior within you will hear your words and be weakened by them."*

### Ancient Samurai proverb

**Please everyone:** if you don't want to do something, say so; if you don't want to go for a drink that day, say so; if you can't or don't want to do something for some reason, don't do it. Take care of feeling good and taking care of yourself and then you will be able to take care of others without problems.

**Leaving for tomorrow what you can do today:** resting and doing "nothing" for a day or a while is not only healthy but also highly recommended. But if it becomes our habit, our way of being becomes routine; we will be losing precious time that we will not be able to recover and that we could have invested in creating, studying, working or achieving.

Exercise:

*Start making a schedule of activities or planning to start incorporating new positive habits into your life. You can start small, and add more throughout the month, so you don't feel pressured or overwhelmed. Surely there are*
*a sport you want to practice, a book you want to read, a dish you would like to learn how to prepare.*

*Fill in your schedule and challenge yourself to evolve and enjoy the change. Because if there's one thing that never changes, it's that everything is constantly changing.*

*Get a new notebook and bring it to life. Write in big letters what you want to achieve. Leave a page for ideas, draft concepts or strategies and budgets. Make a to-do list per page per day. Be concrete, but don't relax or put too much pressure on yourself if you don't achieve what you set out to do. If you accomplish most of the tasks on your daily list, instead of beating yourself up that you didn't accomplish them all, take pride in knowing that you've already done more than you did the day before without a list, without a notebook, and without having started walking.*

*Remember that, if we want to add daily activities to our schedule, the ideal is to start gradually. The best changes are those that come progressively, as they are more likely to last over time. This way, we will not feel like giving up.*

*Add tasks every seven to fifteen days to your schedule. If your goal is to exercise, start with two or three days a week and add days every one to two weeks, so your body and mind can handle it better and you don't feel like giving up.*

Put your life in order and you will be able to appreciate the moments of leisure, rest better and even work, and your productivity will multiply and the results will become visible with speed and weight in your day to day life.

# POSITIVE DISCOMFORT

This concept was consolidated in my mind after understanding the importance of breaking your comfort zone. Or, in other words, stop waiting for the perfect moment to act, and act and make the moment perfect.

We already know that we are creatures of habit, that we like to get home, take off our slippers, have a drink, have dinner, read or watch a movie, or whatever we like to do. We feel comfortable and safe in the routine of habit, it is a way of feeling at ease and there is nothing negative about it, at least in its right balance.

But, however, if that comfortable habit is preventing us from working on ourselves, from taking risks on new projects or making new contacts, or from doing different activities to get different experiences, then it can't be very good.

Everything is good in its right measure, but abusing comfort can be totally harmful if we want to evolve as people or entrepreneurs.

---

*"If you think adventure is dangerous, try routine. It's deadly."*

## Paulo Coelho

---

This phrase makes us see a different perspective from what we are used to.

Again, of course, we all love to be comfortable at home or with some situation, task or business that we have already mastered. But the eagerness to want to improve or the desire to reach our limit and surpass it is a very positive and rewarding thing.

We must realize that most of the knowledge we gain comes from experience and, mainly, that knowledge is gained from bad experience, because that is when we learn the most.

Everything in life is enjoyment or learning, so why not use this information to our advantage? Let's try to fail often! And I'm not saying let's fail on purpose, but rather let's try new ideas, let's try new projects, let's fail, let's learn, let's evolve.

---

*"If you want to succeed, double your error rate."*

## Thomas Watson

---

Successful people talk about the importance of failures, the alleged failures that we criticize so negatively. But they are no such thing. They are excellent opportunities to learn, improve and keep trying. Nobody or almost nobody succeeds the first time, and the mere fact of being able to try again is a privilege. So let's take a breath, think about what we could improve on the next shot and go for it!

As a graphic example, let's think about the moment we want to go to the gym or to exercise:

*The day before we self-motivate ourselves and convince ourselves that this is what we want to do, we go to sleep thinking about starting the day or the week to the fullest, and when we wake up? We get lazy, something hurts or we find a thousand and one convincing excuses not to do it finally.*

---

*"Whoever wants to do something finds a means, whoever wants to do nothing finds an excuse."*

## Arabic proverb

---

It seems to have become an obligation, rather than a desire. And that takes all the fun out of it, doesn't it?

It is extremely difficult for us to ignore the mind and leave the safety of the sofa or comfort to do something that requires minimal effort, even if, in doing so, it gives us tremendous satisfaction and makes us feel fulfilled and positive. But, in my opinion, it is the fact of doing something different or leaving the comfort zone that causes us to reject it.

However, during the exercise, five or ten minutes after starting, we feel great, our mind is relaxed and stress-free, we feel the blood pumping throughout the body, filling it with energy and when we finish, we are champions!

Exercise:

*Think about what tasks you usually perform throughout the day but with reluctance or lack of motivation. We are going to change that perception and attitude so that you can do them with motivation and good energy. Imagine what could happen if we do everything this way: with a positive attitude, your world changes radically.*

*It is very important to reaffirm and convince ourselves that we do this for pleasure, not for duty or obligation. We can even affirm it out loud several times before doing the activity.*

*For example, remember to say out loud: I want to swim, I like it very much, it feels good, and then I feel fulfilled and proud, in addition to improving my health and my physique. Insist: "I want to swim", not "I have to swim". Repeat it often to reaffirm this positive feeling of self-improvement. This way, every time we feel lazy at the thought of doing a certain activity away from the couch or comfort, we will remember that it is good for us, how good we feel while doing it and how, at the end, we feel proud and satisfied with the effort invested.*

*"Every day do something that scares you."*

## Eleanor Roosevelt

I'm not talking about parachuting out of an airplane. Or I am. I am talking about taking risks, accepting the insecurity and uncertainty that comes with doing something new or unknown. I am talking about trying, changing, walking on a different path. Maybe we "fail", because we are new in that habitat, or not, maybe we will find something different that will open our minds and give us what we have been looking for so long and needed the most.

*"If you are looking for different results, don't always do the same thing."*

## Albert Einstein

Find your rhythm, and you will see that creating a better version of you is not only not scary, but one of life's most exciting and rewarding things.

To be able to propose something and achieve it is to materialize our thoughts in real life. It is making the intangible tangible. It is magic. And life is pure magic.

# HELP SOMEONE TODAY

*"Rivers do not drink their own water, trees do not eat their own fruit. The sun does not shine for itself and the flowers do not spread their fragrance for themselves. Living for others is a rule of nature.*

*Life is good when you are happy, but life is much better when others are happy because of you. Our nature is service. He who does not live to serve, does not serve to live."*

**Jorge Bergoglio**

I once heard the phrase, *"If we all helped our neighbor, no one would need help"*. It seems to me that it says a lot about what we could achieve if we were more empathetic and sensitive and learned to work more collectively than individually.

From an early age, we were taught to compete with others, get better grades, win at sports, have better toys, and so on. We spend our whole lives putting labels on ourselves that we believe define our identity, but, in my opinion, separate us from the rest of the people around us. Of course, there is such a thing as healthy competition, but if it is ever not practiced, it is because we focus more on what separates us than what unites us. If someone belongs to a soccer team, a specific political ideology, a religion, a specific social class, a gender, a country, does that make them better than someone who does not "belong" to that person? No, not at all. It just makes you different. And that's a good thing. Look at nature, bursting with color and variety, difference and life. That's partly what makes it beautiful, its varied richness and diverse abundance. It is obviously good to be different; indeed, I would say that recognizing the differences and quirks in each of us and embracing them is essential and makes us free and strong.

But if we highlight our differences when we compare ourselves with other people, we are building invisible barriers that separate us from them, and thus we consolidate our difference as something negative and close the door to our evolution, instead of being aware of the wonderful opportunity we have to learn.

If we only get together with people who are "the same" as us, we will learn little. If we get together with those of different age, ideology, culture, religion, country, gender, it will be an incredible opportunity to expand our vision and learn new things.

I believe that this is the main problem why, habitually and automatically, we do not tend to be more open with others: because of our unconscious rejection of the different, the unknown and our intense "love" of comfort. And you don't have to go far to see it or to find a case of differences between countries, religions or cultures. In the same country, those in the capital treat those in the suburbs differently, or those in the suburbs treat those in the capital differently, or those in a village confront the village next door and reject each other. It is a shame, but it happens today in the 21st century, and all for fear of the unknown, of not being in control of the situation, of changing our customs or ideals. In this way, new knowledge entry is prevented, progress is prevented, and evolution is prevented.

Don't let your mind tell you what to do, don't listen to it if what it has to give you is distrust or fear. Follow your heart and your natural instinct, the one that we have ignored for so long but that is still there and pushes you to do new things, to risk and to always learn.

*"Our main purpose in this life is to help others. And if you can't help them, at least don't hurt them."*

## Dalai Lama

It's as simple as that. It helps without thinking, naturally. And if we have to make an effort at the beginning because it doesn't come naturally, let's force the machine then. All for a good cause. It may not make a big difference to you, but it could mean a lot to that person. You've already improved their day or their journey, and all with a simple gesture.

And by changing yourself, you help the world change for the better. It's the little things that make life worth living. Small things, added to other "small" acts, can do immense things.

There is no small good deed, no good deed without reward. To a greater or lesser extent, all that good energy and intention you gave will come back to you in one way or another, it is inevitable. And so, the cycle of humanity, of empathy and fellowship, will run its course and will never be lost. Let us infect others with good, let us allow everything around us to be kindness and good intentions. In this way, we create our own world, our own rules.

Don't let the storm make you forget the sun. And be the sun for someone today. Be the one who makes a difference, be the one who surprises and makes them doubt the injustice of the real world, be the one who restores faith in humanity these days. Let's sow a little fantasy, joy, affection and good manners on the ground where our human family walks, and "without apparent reason", without reason or festivity, without fear of divine punishment for not acting properly. Let's do it because it is the right thing to do, because treating others well triggers good things, because it is an imperative need to help our equals, and by equals, I mean different, and by different, I mean equal. Let us help each and every person who crosses our path, whenever we see that we can help or improve their life with a simple smile, with a kind word, with a sincere interest, with a detail. No token of affection falls on deaf ears; it is a seed that will make the tree of humanity grow and will only bear fruits of understanding, respect, companionship and love.

Exercise:

*Be attentive to your daily life; there is someone around you who can improve their day thanks to the help you can give them by giving them a smile, helping them push the car or holding the door. Don't miss an opportunity to leave your comfort zone and help someone today momentarily. You will make that person's day and you will have taken a step closer to understanding that we are all equal and equally deserving of love, respect and opportunity. Smile at anyone you feel most deserves it and anyone who doesn't, too. Dazzle every person you meet with your kindness.*

In the end, without realizing it, you will have forgotten your daily problems, discomforts and worries by focusing on others and their well-being. And that is priceless.

# LESS IS MORE

From an early age our brains are bombarded with advertisements of cars, beautiful people, colognes, beautiful people again, more cars, etc. They are a visual stimulus that, as we talked about in the chapter "High Vibration", are deposited little by little in our subconscious modifying its nature and making us hungry to consume, change, buy, throw away... and buy again. Don't misunderstand me. Change is good, especially if you don't feel comfortable being the way you are or being where you are. But if you have seemingly "everything", there will be a time when you fall into routine and boredom or demotivation and stop appreciating and valuing all the good things around you. Then, just by the desire to feel that novelty and enthusiasm again, you may decide to throw it all away and abandon what took you so many years to build. You reject what you love and what you have had for so long, just to have what you "want" momentarily or what you think you want. And all, thanks to the constant bombardment of stimuli that encourage your dissatisfaction and stir up your discontent and anxiety. That is the kind of change I was referring to, although more than change, I think it is involution.

Also in the chapter *"Pleasure for the sake of pleasure"*, we talked about how important it is not to base our "happiness" on passing and superficial pleasures, since we will always depend on an external source to feel again that momentary "well-being" that pleasure gives.

Again, I want to clarify that pleasure is not bad if we do not base our life on it or make it an abuse and an obsession. Sex, alcohol, money, everyone will know how to handle them. But if that which in specific moments can give us temporary relief, we turn it into our only source of relief; there will come a time when it will give us the opposite. The day will come when our "well-being" will be only physical and our mind will be empty, unmotivated and sad.

I know first-hand cases of people who were born into a millionaire family and after 30 are depressed, alcoholics, or with worse vices.

Let us reflect on these words because for me, they are a very important piece of advice:

*"Happiness is not in having what you want, but in wanting what you have."*

### Confucius

Overstimulation and especially the obsession or desire to get more and more material possessions leads nowhere. Or, rather, it leads nowhere worth being. If we want to have more and more, in the end, we value nothing. *"And we will lose the moon by going around counting stars."*

**It is not about thinking that we have less but about feeling that we have everything.**

Even if we still desire something else or want to accomplish more goals, we must constantly be grateful so that we do not forget where we come from and the great abundance that surrounds us and of which we are a part on a daily basis.

There will always be someone who has less than us and will be happy; there will always be someone who has more and will be unhappy. That is why we must be aware of how fortunate we are simply to be here and now, reading this book, in a private moment of calm and inner search, investigating, evolving and understanding more of this wonderful and complex mechanism in which it has fallen to us to live, our being.

If we knew all the tricks, it would lose the fun, if everything was easy, it would be boring; if we had all the treasures in the world, a different "love" every night, all the money, sex and vices you could imagine, nothing would be worth it. Nothing would be worth the effort and sacrifice, the time and will it takes to achieve it. So how could we value it?

There is a saying that goes: *"What comes fast, goes fast",* or what is the same, what came easy, just as easy or even easier, will go away. If it did not take us time to get it, if we did not invest part of our energy and dedication, if it was not "hard" and we had to focus and be conscious, giving up leisure time to get it, then it will not mean anything. In our head will be set a mental marker as if to say, *"bah, I got it fast and easy, I can have it whenever I want and, like this one, many more".* Then you think that, if it doesn't work for you, you can take another and another without stopping to enjoy the experience, without valuing anything.

For this reason and many others, I decided to make a chapter called *"Less is more".* Although it may seem like a simple concept that can be summarized in a couple of lines, it is often difficult for us to assimilate.

"Less is more" does not mean thinking that you have little, it means feeling that what you have is enough, it means being grateful for what you have and are, being aware of how much beauty and love surrounds us.

That's why I use the word "think" when I write "think you have little", and that's why I use the word "feel" when I write "feel that what you have is enough", because thinking doesn't have to imply consciousness on your part, we all think every day without having to be part of that "action", thinking happens most of the time without us having to do anything.

But feeling, that's another matter. Most of the time it is a decision, even if we don't see it that way. First, I think, consciously or unconsciously, then I feel, and then comes a sensation. It requires more participation on our part.

If a thought arises spontaneously in our mind and we pay attention to it for a certain time, we choose, yes, we choose, to feel a certain way and that gives us a feeling, which can be good or bad depending on the thought and the power of our imagination.

Exercise:

*Look at everything around you: do you have a home, a family, a job, friends, a partner, do you eat more than once a day, do you have health, free time, can you exercise, read, go to a new restaurant? Then you already have much more than 75% of the population.*

*Take a deep breath and say out loud slowly, as you feel the power of the words of gratitude you are reading:*

*I appreciate this moment and the experience I am receiving. Thank you.*

*I have a house, food, health, work, friends, and love. I am surrounded by abundance and I am very fortunate, I don't need anything to be happy. I am already happy. I live happy.*

*I smile as I breathe. And I give my all so that those around me are happy too.*

*Thank you world. Thank you air. Thank you sun. Thank you life.*

I hope from the bottom of my heart that you feel the power of these words in your being. Remember that you can repeat these affirmations whenever you want, or others that you invent yourself to reinforce something in your mind. The power is not only in words, but in their message and the intention with which they are read.

You are powerful. You have in your mind the power to give peace to your soul in many ways and one of them you have discovered now. Never forget your power.

We are privileged. As I was saying, boredom and depression are problems of the first world, of the West. Only here, we are so distracted by so many external stimuli that we are not able to stop and breathe slowly and deeply for a few minutes, to feel our body, to slow down our mind, to cultivate our peace.

# ABUNDANCE

Abundance may sound like possessing great wealth, living in luxury and squandering money. But it is also a spiritual term to define all the good we receive and surround us. In my opinion, being aware of how fortunate we are made us grateful, feeling that gratitude makes us happy, and feeling happy is the key to abundance.

For someone from the city, being in the middle of nature may seem boring, lacking the action and frenzy of the city. But maybe for someone else from the same city, the same neighborhood, even the same family, being in a mountain can be a totally incredible experience. Same birthplace, almost the same DNA, and what changes? The eyes that admire the landscape, the perspective and the perception.

What we focus our attention on expands our life. If we focus on the bad, the universe will get the message that we like the bad and more bad things will appear. On the other hand, if we look at the positive and appreciate all that we are and all that surrounds us, we will live in abundance.

If I walk through the park, I can be remembering the bad day I had at work, how little I want to go back tomorrow, how much time I still have to finish that complicated project... And suddenly, maybe we step on a dog excrement or we get a scare when crossing the street because we were not attentive and did not look at both sides of the road before passing, or they call us and give us bad news. It seems to be done on purpose. Seriously, one bad thing happens to you and it seems that behind it comes another and another and another... But it's not like that, it's our filter that only focuses on the bad and forgets about all the good things around.

Perhaps, if we hadn't been so distracted by our thoughts while we were walking through the park, we would have noticed what a fantastic day it was, or those curious flowers that had grown on the side of the road, or that little girl playing with her dog and dying with laughter every time she brought him the ball again.

Life is what you want to see. It is a mixture of perfectly structured spontaneous events coupled with your attitude and way of seeing things.

Attitude is everything, they say, and they are not wrong. The same event that may be boring or unpleasant for one maybe a wonder and a real pleasure for another. Yes, we are different, but if I am not able to observe, appreciate and be grateful for the immense abundance that surrounds me, hadn't I better learn to think differently in order to see it?

---

*"They tell of a wise man who one day
was so poor and miserable
that he only sustained himself
with some herbs that he picked.
Could there be another, he said to himself,
poorer and sadder than I?
and when his face turned
he found the answer, seeing
that another wise man was picking up
the herbs that he threw.*

*Complaining about my fortune
I was living in this world, and when I said to myself, "
Is there any other person
of more troublesome fortune?
Pious you have answered me.
For, returning to my sense, I
find that
you would have gathered
my sorrows*

*to make them joys".*

## Pedro Calderón de la Barca "La vida es sueño" (Life is a dream) 17th century

What for some are leftovers, for others are food. What for you may be discomfort, for another may be learning. What for some is hell, for others is effort and will. And, if you cannot, like others, appreciate the abundance that surrounds us after reading these verses, then be another. Change. Meditate, evolve, learn, and transform yourself. Be another. Be the one you want to be. The one who enjoys a rainy day as much as a sunny one, the one who brings a smile to those who need it and changes their day. The one who helps without expecting to receive anything. I know who you want to be, but if you are not yet, start now because there is hardly time to realize that what is gone is what is really worthwhile. The time, the experiences, the love, the laughter, the friendship, the life. If you're not here to live it, someone else will. But it won't be you; it will be someone else. So if you don't like this day, no matter how it looks, if you're sick of your job and yet you're still at it, if you can't laugh out loud for no reason, if you can't smile at a stranger, then be someone else.

Abundance exists in all forms and levels. It is food, it is energy, it is love, it is music, it is joy, and it is life. It is having an incredible conversation with someone you have just met and feeling like you have known them before. It is walking down an unfamiliar street and discovering a foreign food restaurant and walking in to discover exotic flavors. It's discovering a new singer and loving almost all of their songs. Abundance is traveling to a country you didn't know, noticing that you feel at home and would like to live there. But none of this will happen if you are not able to savor that abundance, if above you only see the black clouds. Sometimes they are not even there, but we create them anyway. Because we think, act and materialize. So, we are creators of our reality to some extent. They never taught us to write our destiny in school, they did not know how to teach us to draw our life, but it is never too late to learn.

Exercise:

*Come home after work or after finishing your day and sit down in a comfortable place. Take a couple of slow, deep breaths. Open your favorite notebook or notebook and write down the date of the day. Write down two good things that happened to you today, something you were told or felt, something that happened or noticed. Something different and positive. If you feel confident, write more, as many as you want. Now read them again; what feeling do they give you?*

Repeat this exercise every day for a month. In this way, we educate the mind to focus on the good things in our lives. In this way, we eliminate negativity and depression or dissatisfaction. In this way, we learn to be aware of the infinite abundance that surrounds us and of which we are constantly a part.

# NEUTRAL INTERPRETATION

When we witness someone's actions or are told a story that has just happened, it is inevitable or, rather, almost impossible not to judge them. We find it good, right, wrong, or horrible, but it does not usually leave us indifferent. We have to express our opinion. It is our way to empathize or differentiate ourselves, expose our ideals, and defend our identity. And that's totally valid. But there is something very interesting to think about this:

When we create something good, that is to say, when in our mind we establish that a fact or a concept is correct, or that to achieve something determined is ideal, without wanting to, we are also creating something bad, because we give life to its opposite. That is, the absence of that good thing we would like to achieve is something negative. For example, if we wanted to finish our career (something good) and finally we could not do it (something bad) because our father got sick and we had to start working before finishing our studies, we will feel bad. That which was so good was not fulfilled or we did not achieve it and then we do not feel good. Unconsciously, we have programmed our mind with the belief that it is wrong for us to get the opposite of what we wanted or to not get the good thing we wanted. *"I didn't get that job I wanted," "I'm thirty years old and I'm not married yet," "I wanted to have had children before I was thirty-five," and* so on.

Obviously, these are frustrating events that anyone would find upsetting or temporarily blocked. There are also acts that are indisputably evil and have no other way of looking at them, crimes, murders, sexual assaults and a long, etc. There is no denying that. But the facts of our day to day lives are what matter to us here.

The concept of neutral interpretation is simple to explain and complicated to apply because we must face the human mental conditioning that has taken its toll on us for centuries, so it will be necessary to be very aware of our unconscious reactions.

Neutral interpretation consists of remaining before our personality and our judgment, where something is neither good nor bad; it simply IS. And that, believe me, is already good. It means staying away from the mind and its delusions and not allowing it to develop judgments that lead us nowhere or lead to nothing good.

For example, if I am driving down the road and a person crosses the road dangerously, I would use my horn to warn him acoustically. If all of a sudden then, he changes lanes and brakes, gets to my height and shouts at me, insults me or makes aggressive hand gestures, I could follow his energetic current and shout at him and insult him as well, making me an accomplice of his bad behavior and paying myself, at least energetically, for the consequences of his mistakes. Finally, it could end up even worse because during the anger, I am not 100% focused on the road and I am putting myself at risk of causing an accident.

But instead, we could also take a deep breath or smile and make a gesture expressing our apologies, even if it was not even our fault, and continue on our way without further complications. That way, we would not allow their bad energy to affect and contaminate us, and we would be able to continue on our way unharmed and with our vibration intact. Nothing can affect you if you do not allow it to. As the popular saying goes, *"it is not he who wants to offend but he who can"*. Well then, do not allow them to offend you. It is not about being defensive, about resisting. It is about accepting and letting go. To identify that behavior as unhelpful and let it go where it came from.

*"The monk and his disciple were walking down the street when suddenly a man ran by and brutally struck the master, knocking him to the ground. Master! -cried the alarmed disciple as he helped his master to his feet, "Are you all right?*
*The old monk calmly stood up, shook the dust from his robes and resumed his march without any reaction or complaint on his part. But master! -the student exclaimed loudly, "who was that man? You didn't even look at him, you don't even know who he is or why he did it! It's your problem, not mine," the teacher replied calmly.*

### A tale from the Zen tradition

The problem is not ours until we decide to make it ours by reacting negatively. We do not have to react, we have to act, accepting what happens and letting it pass by or ignoring it, and sometimes, it is not even necessary to act.

All this has nothing to do with letting yourself be humiliated or allowing yourself to be abused, far from it. In life, it is almost never black and white, just different shades of gray.

*"If you have 86400 euros and someone steals 60 from you would you throw away the other 86340? No, wouldn't you? Now imagine that, instead of 86400 euros, you have 86400 seconds, exactly the seconds a day lasts. So tell me would you throw away the 86340 seconds you have left after someone wastes 60 seconds of your time with their bad attitude or intentions?"*

### Text extracted, translated and versioned by Marc Levy, from his book "Et si c'était vrai (And if it were true)" year 2000.

Think about it this way the next time you feel full of anger or rage because of someone's bad attitude or abuse, and meditate deeply and sincerely on whether it is worth wasting your whole day angry or bitter just because someone took 60 seconds of your time with their bad manners, intentions or words.

Exercise:

*Whenever you are beset by bad energy, hear harsh criticism or see your emotional or energetic stability in danger, simply walk away. And whether it is possible or not to walk away, do not interpret it, do not accuse, do not judge. Focus on your breath, feel your body. You can say to yourself:*

"You're not mine, you don't belong to me, I don't want you here."

*Or simply:*

"It doesn't bring me anything next!"

*Or also:*

"Thank you for participating! We'll get back to you!"

You are the creator and the destroyer, the beginning and the end of everything you wish or do not wish to have in your life. Use your thoughts to your advantage and don't let them use you, because believe me, they will if they arrive and don't find someone at the helm of the ship.

# LAW OF ATTRACTION

We are creative beings, I will never tire of repeating it. As we said in the chapter *"High Vibration"*, **thoughts are the raw material to materialize our dreams.** We have the power to turn something ethereal, something without form, into something tangible and physical in the real world. If we decide to study a career because we want to be a journalist, for example, we will go to class for years, study, take exams and finally get the degree. We will look for a job and eventually end up working as journalists. We've made it. Something that only existed in our head became real through our actions.

The vast majority of us are unaware of this great power. We were not shown it as children or taught how to use it. However, throughout our existence, there are moments when you realize that there is something more influencing your life than just chance or random events. You were thinking about a long-time friend you hadn't spoken to in weeks, and suddenly he called you. Or you meet someone for the first time, and the next day you meet them again somewhere else, or you are looking for a job and in a conversation someone offers you a unique opportunity. Some call it chance, others causality, **Carl Jung called it** *"synchronicity"*.

Synchronicity is the universe's way of saying yes. It's how you know you're in the right place, at the right time, with the right person. If you take full advantage of that moment, you will surely gain a valuable lesson or be able to teach or help someone in some way. When you are left thinking *"how is that possible, what a coincidence!"*

Then it is the ideal time to be fully aware and alert to what is happening. Something special may happen, an opportunity to develop yourself, evolve on a work or emotional level, or both.

Our subconscious governs our life. The accumulation of experiences, memories, stimuli and other factors, program our unconscious side during our stay on Earth. All this information creates a unique version of our identity, an individual perception that makes us react in one way or another when faced with day-to-day events. This series of impulses or automatic reactions is unconscious and affects our perspective of the world definitively, altering how we see what surrounds us.

If we had a hard childhood, we may distrust someone who wants to open up to us or who treats us well or, on the contrary, perhaps at the slightest opportunity we see to trust someone, we do it blindly and without waiting for that trust to be generated naturally, which may cause the other person to get scared and run away.

A large part of our life is absolutely governed by the unconscious, and we don't realize it because it has always been that way. But what if we could naturally influence the subconscious and thus create a more positive and happier version of ourselves? That is possible, but like almost everything good in life, it requires effort and commitment.

*"Utopia is on the horizon. I walk two steps, it moves two steps away and the horizon runs ten steps further. So what is utopia for? That's what it's for, it's for walking.*

## Eduardo Galeano

We are not going to achieve the best version of ourselves in the blink of an eye overnight. If that were the case, it would be worthless and we would probably get bored after a while and go back to the way we were before. Good wine takes years to mature. A good relationship is consolidated with time, affection, understanding and details. A resistant and leafy tree is watered with love and time, not only with water. So, let's not expect to be able to change all our behavioral or perception problems with lightning speed.

There was a phrase I wrote some time ago that I like to remember when I have a negative thought or that motivates me to focus on things that are unfair or that do not bring me anything:

> *"There is no such thing as perfection. If you accept it, everything becomes perfect."*
>
> ## Chris Diaz

What should be perfect is not the world around us but our way of observing and appreciating it. We all make mistakes, even in nature things happen that, from our perspective, may seem cruel and devastating. But the world is not how it is, but how you look at it.

**If you change the way you look at the world, your world will change.**

Exercise:

*If we want to achieve a large or long-term goal, it is very useful and important to mark those small tasks or goals necessary to reach the final objective. Step by step, we will achieve great things. The best way to get somewhere is to start walking. Enjoy the enriching journey of learning and personal growth. Few people are brave enough to venture along this path to evolve in different aspects.*

*1° On a page of your new, shiny and powerful notebook, write the title of what you would like to achieve, something big. Your dream job, life plan, sports goals, ideal house, financial freedom... now write down under that important title all the small goals or activities necessary to get there. Don't skimp on the details. Now, you know that what you want to achieve has great value and you will appreciate it when you get it. Go little by little, day by day, fulfilling the small goals in the notebook to get closer to your big goal. If you feel you are not making progress in one part, try new strategies and different ways to achieve it: study, research, consult those who already know or are succeeding in something similar and version what they did to achieve it. By putting it down on paper, we are already starting to materialize it to make it real.*

*2° Repeat out loud daily what you want to achieve and why you want it as if you had already achieved it. Imagine yourself in that situation, with your goal accomplished, in detail. Visualize how you would dress, how you would talk, what house you would have and most importantly, how you would feel. Write it down and repeat it aloud as if you already have it. Without hesitation, with passion and will. Combine these techniques and you will achieve everything you set your mind to. Be grateful for all this process of growth and feel the creative power that emanates from within you. That is the way to attract whatever you desire into your life, becoming its magnet.*

You can achieve anything you set your mind to with will and perseverance.

# THINK LESS, FEEL MORE

Notice how, every time you receive good news and celebrate it, time flies by, you come up with the best jokes, you are grateful and happy, and you share that good energy and affection with everyone around you. There is no time for the mind to interrupt with its constant whispering and blurt out meaningless thoughts. We are too busy living in the now, in the present or, which is the same thing, we are thinking less and feeling more. And don't you think it would be amazing to live every moment of your life like this, or at least most of it?

That is quite possible if we concentrate and observe in which moments of our life we are on *"autopilot"* and in which moments we totally decide what we are doing. If we are distracted, thinking about our worries or problems, looking at our cell phone or television, the mind is working for us; we have hardly any decision in its operation. Our appreciation of reality diminishes and we enter a loop of indifference and apathy and, above all, of little creativity and productivity.

If, on the contrary, we are focused on a task, a sport, an interesting job or a deep talk with someone, we are living in the now; we are being more SOUL than MIND, we are thinking less and feeling more. It is a kind of meditation in action, as we do not allow the mind to pollute the moment with its usual interferences and we give free rein to our passion and creativity. That is my way of looking at it and the one that has helped me the most to focus my energy on living in the present, which is where everything happens.

If you dedicate part of your energy to educate your mind, you will heal your soul.

When we realize that thoughts arise spontaneously in our head, without reason or trigger, and that many times they do not bring us anything or lead us to act or react in a negative way, we are being conscious. We are feeling. We are more soul than mind. That is the magical moment when we realize that our unconscious mind does not represent our identity, but our conscious mind does. Since it is with it that we have choice, it is by being conscious that we make the best decisions when we combine reason and experience, thoughts and feelings, mind and soul. If everything were impulse without consciousness, we would still be animals and have to kill each other to survive.

Perhaps, sometimes we cannot choose what to think about since the dish is already served on the table, but we can choose what to "feed", that is, we can choose which thoughts to pay attention to, which ones are worth developing and give them a time that we will never get back.

Let's look at it this way: I am thinking about something that is not good for me, something that has not even happened perhaps, a fear or a worry. When we imagine something, the immense power of our mind makes it feel as if it is already happening, it puts every cell to work on that thought and the whole feeling, negative or positive, floods and governs us. The system fills up with hormones produced by the emotions and we stop being aware of what we are thinking and enter a loop. Don't let that happen. Cut the process off when you want to. We are mostly emotional animals, not rational, because logical reasoning disappears when an emotion has reached our head.

Look at the negative emotions that have caused so much destruction on the planet: greed, the inexhaustible thirst for money and corruption, religious fanaticism, power, abuse and control, envy... they lead to nothing good and consume their owner to the core.

Exercise:

*When some thought that does not please us knocks at the door, do not worry, do not feel, do not give it value or meaning, do not pay attention to it more than necessary. As it came, let it go. Draw your attention to something else. Up to this point, we have explained different techniques throughout this book to focus your mind on the now and I believe you already have the necessary tools to start achieving it. It all boils down to this: when some negative unconscious thought comes to you, be positively aware. When you THINK something bad, DO something good. In other words, don't let your mind take you for a ride; take it wherever you want it to go. Use techniques described in previous chapters: touch the wall and feel it, or your body or clothes and see how they feel, focus on your breathing, sing, hum, talk out loud, say "I'm not interested, thank you and good day", exercise, write in your power notebook "nothing bad stays with me". And suddenly, faster than you can realize, it will be gone. You have a few ways to achieve this; choose the one that resonates or appeals to you, the one that suits you or makes sense to you.*

Not all the techniques for living in the present are here, nor are they the only ones that exist. Surely there are many more and you may discover or invent more along the way. The techniques described here are the ones that worked for me and continue to help me today. With all my heart, I hope they lighten your weight and allow you to fly freer.

Thank you for being here and now.

# FINAL REFLECTION

The journey through this book has concluded, but your inner journey of self-improvement and development has only just begun, or continued to the end of the road.

That is one of the great beauties of life: to be nourished by our environment to improve at all levels. Being able to look inward when we feel that something is troubling us will make us better understand how our emotions, health, mind and soul work.

If we give healthy and positive food to our mind, the repercussions will be positive in many aspects. Our energy and willpower will increase, as well as our concentration and mood will improve. We will also sleep better, have a good day and, in this way, create a cycle of well-being that will improve our life enormously.

In the same way, if we choose well which thoughts to pay attention to so that only those that bring us something positive develop, our mind will be calmer and free of stress and anxiety. We will be able to function better at work, our decision-making capacity will be improved, we will be more positive, etc.

---

*"In the warmth of the campfire, an old Indian was telling his grandson: In our heart there are two wolves fighting. One of them is an angry, violent and vengeful wolf. The other is full of love, gratitude and compassion.*
*The grandson asked, "Grandfather, which of the two will win the fight?" Grandfather replied, "The one I feed."*

### Old Cherokee tale

---

We should not blame ourselves for what we think unconsciously, but we should take responsibility for what we feel, since it requires more participation on our part. The thought may arise on its own, but we allow it to gain strength and develop by giving it our full attention. Choose wisely what you want to see grow in you.

Likewise, our soul also asks for proper "nourishment". By taking care of our mind in different ways, the soul will feel at peace, happy, grateful and we will be able to turn to it when the mind "betrays" us. The soul is our corner, where all is well, where there are no interferences or problems, stress or suffering, and we can reach it when we live in the now without distractions.

Thinking is of the mind; feeling is of the soul. If we choose to embrace and develop only positive thoughts, the soul will give us sensations and feelings of happiness and well-being. It sounds simple, but it can be a bit more complex to put into practice, like everything good in life that lasts over time. Once you discover your true power, life will be an enriching and abundant experience at every step. Don't let the opportunity for better living slip through your fingers.

Remember to breathe deeply and slowly and focus your attention on your body whenever you feel stress or anxiety or overthinking. **The same energy that upsets you is the same energy that can calm you down.** You just have to learn to direct it and use it to your advantage.

## Thank you for choosing my book!!!!

I sincerely hope that you enjoy the journey through the pages of this book and that my experiences can help and motivate you to walk your own path towards personal growth, mental health and happiness.

## Help me to help!

The best way to support me is thanks to a positive review or rating of my book on the page where you got it. It will only take you a few seconds to do it, but it means a lot to me.

Your good rating helps my work reach more people and positively impact their lives, health and well-being.

I wish you a happy journey, peace and abundance,
Chris Zen

Made in the USA
Las Vegas, NV
19 March 2025